I0411722

My Journey to Hell

A Story of Love, Loss and Hope

Geri A. Condon, L.C.P.C.

Dedication

I dedicate this book foremost to my son, Mitchell. He has struggled in ways no human should have to experience. I also dedicate this book to my entire family as we have all lived this tragedy and will forever feel its affects. I love you all.

Forward

I have suffered a tragedy that I hope you will never have to experience. Unfortunately, others before me have, and others to come will, experience similar tragedies. This is written to help those who are struggling to move past a loved one's attempted or successful suicide. In my case, I bring the unique perspective of approaching this topic from both a personal and professional level. I am a parent of a child who attempted suicide. I am also a professional who has studied and counseled those dealing with suicide. My goal in this writing is to combine my shared experiences in a way that will offer hope for your future.

Disclosure

There are similarities common to families who have lost a member to suicide just as there are similarities common to families where a member has survived a suicide attempt. That said, I would never assume to compare the depth of loss and grief of a family who has experienced the tragic loss of a loved one to a family who still has their loved one present in this world. The intent of this book is to point out the warning signs, share the common threads of those who have experienced suicide in their families, whether attempted or to completion, and offer ways to move past the grief. Suicide, as well as attempted suicide, effects family and friends. It often leaves loved ones with a deep sense of hopelessness.

I was working on writing this book for more than a year when the tragic death and suicide of Robin Williams was announced. I cite this tragic loss of a celebrity who brought so much happiness into people's lives because, I believe, his death brought new awareness about depression. If a celebrity with fame, financial and professional success can struggle with depression to the point of suicide, clearly it can happen to anyone and, in fact, it does.

Table of Contents

My Story – Part I

That Day   **9**

My Background   **12**

Failure   **14**

My Baby Boy   **16**

Hospital Round 1   **20**

Suicide in the Making   **25**

Day of Disintegration   **33**

The Story Goes On & On & On…   **37**

Always on the Look Out   **39**

What You May Experience – Part II

Psychiatric In-Patient Treatment   **42**

Suicide and Addiction   **44**

Family Dynamics   **47**

Perceptions and Support   **55**

Stages of Grief   **58**

Guilt   **60**

Statistics   **62**

Warning Signs   **64**

Getting Help   **67**

And Here We Are Now   **70**

Conclusion & Final Thoughts **74**

Thank You   **78**

References   **80**

My Story - Part I

That Day

I hate to start with a cliché but it's the truth: My day began as any other day. Well, I guess that requires some clarification. When I say, 'any other day,' this isn't to say that my days were 'ordinary' by everyone's standards. I woke up, read the paper, showered, dressed and headed to City Hall for my first meeting of the day. As an alderwoman, I was there to review an issue with a department head.

The meeting went a little longer than expected. Even so, afterward, I stopped at a store to do a little shopping. While shopping, a good friend called and told me that her brother-in-law had just committed suicide. As a Licensed Clinical Professional Counselor, calls from friends needing emotional support are not uncommon. Friends know I will offer a compassionate ear to their struggles. We spoke a while, I finished my shopping and headed home to have lunch with my 18-year-old son, unaware, I was about to encounter a family crisis of my own.

Do you know how some of the most monumental moments in your life seem to unfold in slow motion? When you recall them later, no matter how much time has passed, they still appear in your memory that way. I was about a block from my subdivision when I heard police sirens behind me and pulled over to allow the squad car to go around me. At the time, I was on the phone with my mom for her daily "check-in." The phone beeped to let me know I had another call but I let it go to voicemail. Little did I know the Police Chief was calling to inform me of a crisis that was about to change my life, and my families' life, forever. Up ahead, I saw the squad car turn into my subdivision. I remember telling my mom that I had to end our call because I had a bad feeling about what was happening around me. While turning into my subdivision, I saw another squad car coming toward me from the opposite direction. As I turned onto my street and saw several other squad cars in front of my home, I went numb. My heart raced and I felt overcome by a sheer feeling of dread and pending disaster.

As an officer approached the front door of my home, I remember pressing the garage door opener. I pulled into my driveway, but cannot really say whether I turned the car engine off or not. Getting got out of the car, I started running toward the garage. The Deputy Police Chief grabbed me and told me that I had to let the officers go into my home and "do their job". I screamed, "Is it Mitchell? Is he ok?" The longest moments of my life were spent waiting for the response to that question.

My Background

As the oldest child and oldest grandchild on both parental sides, living in an upper middle-class family, I grew up in relative comfort and stability. I did well academically, was active in school and, overall, would say that life was good.

After high school, I went on to college and continued that pattern: good grades, poms and student council, joined a sorority and held several leadership positions. I pursued a Bachelor's degree in Political Science. Having enjoyed psychology classes, I earned a minor in that field, as well.

As though fulfilling a plan, I graduated, took a job in state government, married a man I met in college and soon added three children to our family.

When I discovered that working in government wasn't entirely fulfilling, I went back to school and earned a Master's Degree in Counseling. My education in counseling not only provided another career path, it also provided first-hand knowledge of mental health issues. This proved beneficial later when I saw signs of my own son's mental health crisis. The political pull was still strong though and, when an opportunity presented itself, I ran and was elected to the City Council.

The bottom line for sharing this with you is to explain that I was just going about my life, doing the best I could for myself, my family and my community. I served on several community boards and led a bible study. Although I was often told I did too much, I liked my life that way. It kept me busy and generally satisfied. I thought that bad things weren't supposed to happen to me. Those bad things were the things in the newspaper or news broadcasts, not up close and personal in MY life! My busy life was crazy enough!

Failure

Were there any telltale signs I missed? As I look back over 19 years of flashbacks from my son's life, I can honestly answer 'No'. Nothing would have led me to believe that he would become suicidal. Were there any telltale signs of depression or traits of a bi-polar personality? Well, that answer is 'Yes'. As a licensed therapist, I know the signs, but as a mother, I wasn't looking. I was in crisis mode with a son who was struggling. As any professional counselor will tell you, a counselor should never treat family or friends. But, knowing that doesn't lessen the guilt I feel for not acknowledging the signs and bringing my son in for a true diagnosis years earlier.

Guilt is a big factor for most parents when something goes wrong with our children. What I refer to on a regular basis as "mommy guilt" is experienced by most moms to varying degrees. It is a common perception that we are supposed to make everything perfect for our children. Of course, that simply isn't possible and, in fact, allowing our children to struggle a little offers them an opportunity to learn on their own. It's when we see signs of danger or behaviors that are destructive, that we need to act. Even then, as parents, it's difficult to see things clearly because our perspective runs through our parental filter.

My Baby Boy

Like most parents, when my son was born, I thought he was perfect. He slept a lot early on; which we considered a bonus! As he grew, it was very clear that he was social and a flirt! His smile made my heart melt. And his smile had the same reaction on others, too. That charm would later become a tool he would use to get out of troubling situations he often created.

At a First-Grade Parent-Teacher conference, his teacher told us that he was very popular and everyone wanted to play with him. It was obvious to his teacher, even at that age, that he was a bright student. Yet, he was also struggling. By third grade, with his lack of progress in reading, my son was given multiple tests to determine the cause of his learning difficulties. Over the next few years, he was diagnosed with a reading disability, attention deficit and, most troubling, Auditory Processing Disorder. His brain was not properly processing what he heard others say.

The good news was that we now had some understanding of why he struggled with reading and following directions. At the same time, we also learned that he has a very high IQ, which enabled him to compensate for many of his deficits.

He continued to do well socially and received help at school, improving his academic performance. He was very talented in sports: golf, basketball, baseball and soccer. All around, life was going well for him.

Moving on to junior high, he continued to succeed through 6th grade. He even earned a 4.0 and we were so happy for him. Then came 7th grade and our happy and successful son was transformed into someone unrecognizable. His life seemed to come crashing down around him and his difficulties affected the entire family. Did something traumatic happen that year? As his parents, we were unaware of any such cataclysmic events in his life. His grades fell drastically, he got his first of many detentions, and he became sneaky, angry, and defensive. He began losing friends. This was the beginning of a long road of deteriorating relationships, especially with his younger brother.

High school was a disaster. Socially, academically and athletically he was slipping further down a long and frustrating road. It was apparent that, not only was he suffering, but we, his family, were suffering too. I was hoping we could chalk it up to hormones.

We sought out help and brought him in for counseling, the first of a litany of counselors. They always seemed to help, at first, but then the progress would fade away. As a counselor myself, I was disappointed and had to control the urge to step in and do things my way. Of course, that would never work. I was his mom! He did not see me as the professional and I clearly had the skewed vision of a desperate mother with a deep emotional attachment.

The one thing he loved was sports. He excelled athletically. We warned we might deny him access to sports if he didn't bring his grades up – if he didn't show more respect to those in our family. It had little impact. We tried everything we could to motivate him: incentives, punishments, encouragement, guidance, assistance. Nothing seemed to help.

Hospital Round 1

His anger was escalating. One night, in the spring semester of his sophomore year of high school, he lost control and punched a hole into his bedroom wall. He was saying he hated himself and wished he were dead. While he had not made any plans to end his life (A predictor of suicide is suicidal ideation or, simply put, a plan to carry out a suicide), I was not willing to assume he was not suicidal. We called a crisis worker and had him admitted to an adolescence psychological unit at a hospital. Unfortunately, the closest one to where we lived, and the one that had the best reputation, was about 45 minutes from our home.

I was allowed to accompany my son in the ambulance. He was strapped into a gurney: basically immobilized. His father followed in our car. A rainy evening and darkening sky mirrored my emotions as we drove to the hospital. When we arrived, we signed sheaves of paperwork realizing we were basically signing away all our parental rights to a hospital and its doctors. The effect was overwhelming, consuming us with fear. The bottom line, however, was the desire to keep our son safe and to avoid putting him in a position to harm himself. The commitment to the hospital was irrevocable and we were powerless to exercise our parental rights until a doctor approved his release. No sooner had we signed the documents than we were told to say our goodbyes and leave our son to their care. Walking out of the hospital and driving home, my husband and I were devastated. There are no words to describe the magnitude of the guilt and panic that tore at our emotions.

Did we fail our son? Did we fail ourselves? How do we move forward? What do we tell other people? What do we tell our other children? There really were no clear answers. Looking back, I can now say that, no, we did not fail. It just was. It was the life we had before us and the life our son was living. We were all doing the best we could.

While in an adolescent care unit, at least at this facility, we were only allowed to visit twice a week, along with brief phone calls twice a day. In many ways, our home was very peaceful those two weeks he was in the hospital. No fighting, less worrying, just quiet. This was something new for the four of us: his two siblings, his father and me.

The phone calls were short but reassuring. We knew, if nothing else, he was provided for. We could bring him several changes of clothing and his school work on our visits. But, he was not allowed any personal care products. He could have no clothing items with strings. No belts. It all seemed like something out of a movie, not something I would ever experience in real life.

The time spent driving to and from the hospital was filled with anxiety. While we were excited to see our son, we were also full of fear as to what was happening to him and with him. On the way home, we were often depressed. While our son was fighting to gain his footing in a life of depression and anger, his father and I were sinking into our own depression as we watched him struggle. We were embarrassed, ashamed, overwhelmed and completely stripped of the ability to control or influence our son's welfare. We felt isolated and only discussed the situation between ourselves. We also had to compose ourselves around our other children, not wanting to adversely affect them. But, we did see progress.

The most beneficial skill he developed, during his stay in the hospital, was the ability to recognize when he was losing control and how to take a step back and collect himself. There was a room where the adolescents could go to calm down. The only item in the room was a reclining chair. It was a safe place where my son began to learn to calm himself and regain his composure. He could work through and process whatever was causing him to struggle at any given moment (I wish we all had a chair, such as that, in our lives).

When he was released from the hospital, he said he no longer wanted to hurt himself. I was not reassured. I sensed that his anger was percolating just below the surface. However, I did hate the long drives back and forth from the hospital and that was one reason I was happy to have him back at home. I was also cautiously optimistic having him back in our care. At that time, it was what we all wanted.

Suicide in the Making

Time passed but the challenges remained. There were many angry outbursts; school work was ever challenging, and then there were medical concerns. For no apparent reason, my son's lung collapsed. Not just once, but twice. After several surgeries, he was confined to bed rest. The time away from school required private tutoring and special accommodations. Time went on and he finished his senior year of high school with slightly improved grades and a mildly better temperament. Before we knew it, he was off to college.

His college experience began much as it does for many college freshmen. He found it hard to integrate social activities with his scholastic responsibilities. He gained new friends and was active socially. That was a positive. But, his grades after first semester were disappointing. I hoped that, as a freshman, it was just a matter of him finding an appropriate balance.

In August, he had entered college full of excitement and anticipation. By January, he returned for the spring semester feeling apprehensive. His roommate from first semester didn't return to school and our son was forced to build a relationship with a new roommate. Then, my son discovered he was missing personal items from his dorm room. Taking the appropriate steps, the resident assistant was notified of the missing items which were eventually found in the possession of his new roommate. Several other notifications were made with no response from the school. My son began to withdraw from social activities. This included going to the cafeteria for meals. He became afraid to leave his room. Eventually, the campus police were notified and tried to help, but the emotional damage was already done and, with the involvement of the police, came physical threats from the roommate.

Our son was planning on coming home for Easter weekend. We were looking forward to having him home and safe. I knew we would have to discuss his withdrawal from social and academic participation but just having him home would come as a great relief for all of us. That all changed on

Thursday evening, the night before he was to come home. According to my son, he wanted to get out of his room and chose to go to a college bar with a friend. Since he was only 18, making that decision was the beginning of a long and mistake-filled evening.

The police raided the bar and he was charged with: 1. Being under age in a bar, 2. Having fake identification and, 3. Holding a bottle of beer. To add insult to injury, and unbeknownst to us, he had gotten into a fight in January and had failed to appear in court for that offense. When the police realized he had an outstanding warrant, he was handcuffed, arrested and taken to jail. A friend provided his bail so he didn't have to spend the night in jail.

The next morning, he called to share the events of the night before and to tell us he needed money to repay his friend for the bail money. He was very distraught and crying heavily. He said he had been vomiting and could not handle the six-hour ride home for the weekend. I was incredibly sad that he wasn't coming home – sad for myself and sad for him – and very upset about his poor choices. But, I understood how he would feel sitting in a car for a long ride while he was sick. I checked in with him several times over the weekend and was worried about his emotional well-being. I had no idea that his weekend was continuing to deteriorate. Of course, I didn't learn the full story for several days.

Around midnight on that Sunday in April, we received a call from our son. He was still emotional, distraught and obviously overwhelmed. He was depressed and saying things, which I knew, as a professional, suggested the possibility of suicide. We couldn't take any chances with his unstable state of mind. So, my husband and I immediately drove more than six hours to reach him. I hoped he was sleeping and didn't want to call and wake him. But, not calling filled me with the fear of not knowing how he was or what he might do to himself. Finally, we arrived and he was in my arms. I took a huge breath and let out a great sigh of relief. Stepping back to look at him, however, rekindled my anxiety. He looked like a shell of a person.

We packed all his belongings and moved him home that very day. The next week was spent withdrawing him from college, and setting up appointments with a counselor and a psychiatrist. We were keeping a close eye on him. I knew he was struggling to keep control but he was failing miserably.

We tried to carry on with our daily routines; his dad at work, his younger brother to high school, and I continued my community involvement. Organization was always a challenge for him, so I tried helping him organize all the belongings he brought home from college. I began separating the items he would want in his room and those we could box up for when he decided to go back to school or move out on his own. I had every intention of putting away the "college" items and keeping him at home for the next year in the hope he might be ready to return to college. In the meantime, he could continue his education by attending the community college. That was my plan, but not his.

While going through his backpack, I found a crumpled piece of paper. I carefully unwrapped the paper. I didn't think my heart could break any further but it did. The paper was a campus police citation accusing him of smoking cannabis. The date on the ticket was as much, if not more, troubling. It was from the day he called to tell us about the tickets from the bar and the arrest warrant. He had called to say he could not come to see us for the weekend because he was so upset about the tickets that he was vomiting. Yet, he felt good enough to go to another student's room and smoke pot! Unbelievable! I went into an outrage. This was the final straw. All my anxiety, frustration and disappointment rose up inside of me and erupted. It came out as an attack on an already fragile young man. Of course, in my own shattered mind, it was about him not owning up to the whole story and not about the diminished capacity in which he had made these disastrous choices. I was deeply hurt that he chose to stay at school and continue his destructive behavior and not come home to me, his mother, who loves him unconditionally. For my own sake, I needed him home so I could take care of him.

When his dad got home, the three of us gathered to discuss this new information. I'm sad to admit I began yelling and spitting out various accusations while dispensing numerous punishments. Of course, I would never propose that path of action to my clients. But, at that moment, I was pure mother, not the consummate professional. I was just as raw as my son. I suppose I also wanted to keep him home, safe, and sheltered from all of life's temptations. His reaction, as was his pattern, was to claim I was being unfair; it wasn't his fault; denial was running amuck. Again, we heard those familiar words: "I hate my life!" The question was whether he hated it so much that he would try to end it?

Keep in mind, he was only home a few days. And we were on guard, watching for any signs of suicidal ideations. And the words – "I hate my life" – were the words that made the hairs on the back of my neck stand up. How could I be so angry AT him, and scared FOR him, at the same time?

He spent most of the evening in his room. I spent much of the night on the floor outside his room, listening for anything unusual – anything alarming. I was desperately clinging to a fine line between my anger and my fear he would hurt himself.

Finally, he fell asleep and I trudged off to my own bed. The next morning, he was quiet but seemed okay. Of course, 'OKAY' is a relative term. In his case, it meant he wasn't saying that he wanted to harm himself or that he hated himself or that he hated me. Sometimes the quiet is just as alarming as the storm. I guess I was too tired to see 'the quiet' for what it was. Looking back now, as a professional, I realize it was a red flag I should have noticed.

Day of Disintegration

The meeting at City Hall, the store, the call from a
friend about her brother-in-law's suicide, heading
home while ignoring the incoming call and then the
sirens and police cars: it was as though my life was
disintegrating before my eyes. Even today, it unfolds
around me as though in a bad dream with
everything happening in slow motion. I am in a fog
with police going into my home as I'm stopped in
the driveway by the Deputy Police Chief telling me
to let the officers do their job. 'THEIR JOB?!!!' I
am a mom; what about my job? It's my job to help
and protect my son, even if from himself. I feel my
legs collapse beneath me. I'm falling to the ground
as the Deputy Chief tries to distract me by telling me
to call my husband. I am vaguely aware of officers
and paramedics going into my home.

I can't speak clearly but scream for my husband to
just come home – "NOW!" There are so many ways
I could have handled that call better but I was not
operating rationally at that point. I just mumble
something about Mitchell and police.

What was probably only minutes, maybe five, seems like half an hour. I hear the Deputy Chief's radio go off informing him that Mitchell is alive. That is all I can think about at that moment. He's alive! We can and will deal with the rest. He's alive!

My husband arrives home. We're still not allowed inside. Finally, the shell of my son comes out, held up by two strong men. He's only wearing his underwear. He's been crying, his face is pale, he looks scared and he looks lost in his own world. While I struggle for an emotional handrail, something to hold onto, he's led into the ambulance, strapped down and taken to the hospital. We are told after he left that he tried to electrocute himself. He was saved when the circuit breaker tripped. Like zombies, my husband and I drive to the hospital.

We are led to a room in the ER where we find Mitchell strapped to a bed with an armed security guard outside his door. I crumble a little again. I'm holding on to that thin thread of reality.

While we wait for the ER doctor and crisis worker to do their assessments, we try to ask Mitch what happened. He says very little to us but spends quite a while speaking to our priest, whom I had called since he and Mitch have a great relationship. Our priest came immediately. I'm happy Mitch is, at least, talking to someone.

It's obvious he'll need hospitalization and observation for his own safety. The social worker checks for bed availability at area psychiatric hospitals. There are only a few psychiatric in-patient facilities in our vicinity and those that do exist either fail to meet my professional criteria or are over-crowded. Luckily, the case worker finds a place for him at, what I believe, is the best facility in the area – the same hospital he was in before. The difference, this time, is that he's no longer a minor; he's no longer in the pediatric unit. He's an adult who will go to an adult psychological unit.

The process of transfer and admittance seems endless, especially when we're already stressed. Finally, the papers are signed and my son, looking like a lost soul, is led away. I feel myself melting. This is the hardest day of my life. I struggle with simple activities, such as walking, talking and generally functioning. Yet, I still have another child at home and an array of responsibilities that require my attention. Life is moving forward, even when I feel like I cannot.

The Story goes on and on and on…

I want to share with you some of the things that are typical for a person and family facing the hardships of suicide. You see, the struggle my family and I have faced is not unique. Sure, some of the specifics are different, but the patterns and experiences are far too common.

What I can tell you is that my story has not ended. My son faced another attempted suicide several months after the first attempt. That is also common.

Five years later, I wish I could tell you all is well. Like most families dealing with suicide, it's like a shadow we face every day. Yes, there are good times, but the mental illness that has engulfed my son has the potential to cause havoc the rest of his life, and thus the rest of our lives.

After a particularly good month, with Mitchell holding down a good job and in a healthy relationship, my husband made a comment that broke my heart. Upon reflecting on Mitchell's success, he said, "I'm glad this mess is over." I know we were both feeling good about the progress our son was making but I knew better than to get too comfortable with that success. Professionally, I knew that our son had a lifelong illness. There would always be good times and there would always be challenging times. We all hope the good times will outweigh the challenges. But my husband was convinced we were on the road to an endgame with closure on this terrible experience. Professionally, I was not allowed my husband's illusion. I understood bi-polar disorder was a lifelong struggle. I shared with my husband that he should enjoy and cherish this time but to not get too comfortable as Mitchell still had challenges ahead of him – we still had challenges ahead of us. And unfortunately, my warning to Mitchell's father proved correct.

That doesn't mean there is no hope.

Always on the Look Out

As I said before, my son has threatened, explicitly and vaguely, suicide a handful of times. He made actual attempts twice. The first was the attempt by electrocution and the second occurred about two months later.

We knew he was still fragile. We knew he did not react well when he was told "No." As loving parents, there are times when that is simply the only appropriate answer. So, we made him keep his bedroom door open. My husband was in our bedroom and I was in my office, both rooms close to his room. Luckily, we have a great extended family and my niece noticed a troubling post my son had written on Facebook. She told her mom who called my husband. Mitch had posted a goodbye note to a friend and my niece was rightly concerned.

We rushed into his room to find the window open, the screen removed and our son sitting on the ledge of the roof outside of his bedroom window. We got him back inside and calmed him down. He had an excuse ready, claiming he only wanted some time alone outside. I wasn't convinced. After all, he was on a rooftop. I slept on the floor most of the night outside of his open bedroom door again. There was little sleep.

The next morning, the situation of the night before became much more frightening. My husband found a rope, obviously from the night before, on the ground below Mitch's window. It was apparent – he'd planned to hang himself.

While we didn't have him admitted into hospital care again, as a result of this incident, it did cause us to initiate additional services.

Lesson learned: always be on guard; always be alert; always be suspicious.

Sometime later, my son started showing increased signs of depression after a breakup with his girlfriend. I asked him how he was - code for "are you suicidal!?!" He knew I was concerned and why I was concerned. He could recognize the depression settling in but was able to state that he was dealing with the depression and did not feel suicidal. I'm convinced that the ongoing conversations he and I have had about his situation have had an effect on him. He's come to recognize the impact of his attempted suicide, and his illness, on the family.

I have continually shared with him that, if he took his life, my life, as I know it, would also be over. I didn't do this to make him feel guilty. I did it to make sure he knew, or grew to understand, that his life was important to me, as well as to so many others. Many who are suicidal just don't believe their life has meaning. In the midst of their suicidal carousel, they're usually not able to see this. But, when they are more stable, they can and need to hear it.

What You May Experience – Part II

Psychiatric In-Patient Treatment

The psychiatric in-patient floor of a hospital looks, outwardly, like any other hospital setting. The initial difference, you may notice, is that the doors to the unit are locked. The next difference is the visitation schedule. There are only limited days and times when family and friends can visit.

There is a structured schedule for each patient, including sessions that are intended to address their emotional stability. The goal is two-fold: keep them safe and help them learn there are ways, other than suicide, to deal with the struggles of life. For most people, this seems like an easy concept. For people who are depressed, this is a concept they often struggle with on a daily basis.

There are numerous restrictions in a psychiatric ward. Obviously, personal items are at a minimum. Any items they could use to commit suicide – such as strings, belts, etc. – are forbidden. Medications are monitored. All activity is monitored. Group sessions cover a variety of helpful topics but most of the people are currently in no condition to learn and commit to new perspectives when they are merely trying to rebound from whatever traumatic event landed them in the hospital setting in the first place.

Another concern, whether it's in- or out-patient treatment, is the inner circle of the patients. They talk. They share. They learn from each other. Often, this is not a positive learning experience. While they probably feel a sense of bonding through whatever put them in the hospital unit in the first place, this interaction has the potential to expose them to additional and more destructive behaviors. The hope is that the staff is also teaching each patient constructive ways to deal with their struggles.

Suicide and Addiction

When I hear words like overdose, gunshot, or suicide, I don't think of my family. Those are words about what happens to other people, or on TV, but not personally associated with my family or me. I learned about these issues as I trained to help others through such crises. Obviously, it's much easier from the outside helping others than on the inside with your own personal crisis.

One of my best friends had a son who was addicted to heroin. He survived an overdose and prison sentence brought on by this life-debilitating addiction. Days after he was released from prison, he was feeling overwhelmed with the uphill climb ahead of him and sought to 'escape' for a little while. He called on a new friend he'd met in jail and said he had "one hit" of heroin left. He intended to do that one hit and then quit. It was his final hit; he died that night of an overdose in his family's home.

For the people who are unfamiliar with suicide and addiction, they believe there is a weakness in someone who struggles with these issues. It's not true. Both involve a disorder in the human body, primarily a chemical imbalance that confuses the brain.

Often, those who suffer from depression and anxiety find that prescription medications make them feel like zombies. They tend to become over-medicated. However, I have heard from many who suffer from depression that marijuana gives them the greatest relief from their depression. While this may be true, the illegality of marijuana in most states makes marijuana a highly questionable choice. And, as with over medicating, considering the differences between each individual's hormones and body chemistry, it's a challenge to determine the right medication and dosage. When someone is suffering from severe depression they are looking for a quick fix and not a long-term solution. The accessibility of marijuana has led many to turn to pot for relief. For some of these, it proves a gateway drug to other stronger and more addictive drugs.

Recently while facilitating a support group for addicts and their families, I asked the group about their experiences with suicide. About half of the addicts said they had thought of suicide; some had acted on those thoughts. Whether they self-medicate to alleviate depression or their substance abuse was so encompassing, thoughts of suicide appeared as a viable option to escape from their painful lives. Since an overdose is a common means of suicide, it is often hard to determine if an overdose was an intentional suicide attempt or unintentional death from the drug. Regardless there is a correlation.

Family Dynamics

Siblings

It's troubling that, when one child attempts suicide, you have no way of knowing how the other siblings will react. In our case, the older sibling was concerned how her parents were handling the chaos. The younger sibling was angry.

Was I surprised by the anger demonstrated by Mitchell's younger brother? No, I was not. For years, he was exposed to the screaming, fighting, and overall destruction that was left in the wake of his brother's troubled path. One time, he hid in his closet crying. Can you imagine the struggle I endured as the mother of one child who is mentally and physically out of control and threatening suicide and another child who is so scared and confused that he is crying in his closet in a futile attempt to escape the hell he is experiencing in his own home?

As he grew up and became a teenager, he became angry when his brother acted out. When Mitchell's behaviors turned suicidal, his younger brother had no more empathy to offer. He was exposed to the chaos for too long, and simply could no longer show compassion toward Mitchell.

For years, the two couldn't even speak to each other in civil tones. That broke my heart a little bit every day. As my younger son has matured and headed off to college, their relationship has slowly improved, somewhat. I hope time and age will be on their side.

As far as Mitchell's older sister, at times she tries to make a connection with him. She does show compassion, but really that relationship, too, was strained. They yelled at each other often but they maintained a relationship. She was always protective of all her family members. Now, years later, she tries to be both a resource for him as well as an ally. She sees his struggles and recognizes he needs her support. He will often turn to her before he speaks to his dad and me for advice and guidance.

She was always the "caretaker" and really tries to smooth things over for everyone. When she can't, she escapes. Escaping is a common theme she shares with her younger brother. While she chose to live hours away, her younger brother is going to college states away. Quite simply, he will tell you he chose a school farther away to put distance between himself and his brother. While I understand, again, my heart is broken.

Many friends, and even family members, have trouble understanding the relationships between these siblings. In all honesty, unless you've experienced the turmoil that my children have gone through, or some similar crisis, you just can't accurately predict how you would react. Many have criticized how the three treat each other, especially how indifferent, defensive and angry the youngest is toward his brother. I have seen both sides, up close and personal, and I do not fault either child. For both, it's a life and a childhood I wouldn't wish on anyone. That said, my children are all doing the best they can. We try, as often as possible, to do things as a family unit. Beyond that, and as they reach adulthood, I cling to the hope that, with maturity, these bonds can unite them.

As for other families going through a similar crisis, there are no rule books or guidelines on how the other children will respond. They each need to find their own way to cope and process and, eventually, progress.

Extended family - An Uncle and An Aunt React

It's often surprising how each person adjusts and deals with tragedy. By and large, our extended family has served as a source of support and comfort, not only for Mitchell, but also for us, as parents, and his siblings. That said, I've seen two extremes in the way extended family members react.

Sadly, at the time of Mitchell's first suicide attempt, his father and I were planning to attend a wake for a friend who had just passed away from cancer. This man was a community leader and well-liked and respected. He had a lovely family and much to live for.

A couple days after the wake and Mitchell's suicide attempt, a family member made an off-hand comment to my husband. It was something to the effect of how sad it was that a great man like "Bob" had died when someone like Mitch was trying to kill himself. I can't believe that he meant it to come off that way, as though he were comparing the value of their lives - Mitch had survived while Bob, who had so much to offer society, had not. That said, I know he is glad Mitchell is alive and surely wasn't wishing him to end his life. My husband and I recognized we were very sensitive but, at the time, his comment hurt us deeply.

What I've learned is that, if you haven't gone through this, it's unlikely you can understand how much pain such comments can cause.

Another of Mitchell's relatives had a different reaction to his suicide attempts. Mitch and his aunt were close and she tried her best to connect with him. She went out of her way to talk to him, take him to movies and, overall, to look after him. She tried to inspire love and hope. Her presence in his life, then and now, has served as a constant bright light for my son. I will forever be grateful to her for the support she offered Mitchell. While I consider this a priceless gift for Mitchell, I still realize that she hasn't lived the constant hell that we have as we struggled to cope with the chaos and desperation. While she's a great resource for my son, she couldn't possibly understand the turmoil in which her brother and I have struggled. On occasion, she has told us we need to "lighten up on him." Yes, he struggled with depression but that does not excuse him from following the household rules and his responsibilities to himself, his employment, his education and his family. While some degree of latitude was necessary, enabling him would not help him learn to cope with depression and his bi-polar disorder. It wouldn't give him the tools to succeed in the real world.

Living with Mitchell, and his mental illnesses requires us to walk a fine line. To excuse all his poor choices merely enables him, and I refuse to do that. Certainly, compassion and some discretion are required in our parenting.

Grandparents

Rightfully so, all his grandparents were concerned. Each grandparent had a slightly different view but they all showed him love and support. They did, however, see the negative effects he was having on the rest of the family. They all did their best, each with their unique ability to be supportive of him and our entire family.

Spouse

Statistically speaking, many marriages end in divorce when a couple faces traumatic experiences, especially the death of their child. I knew this and knew that going through this experience with my husband would either strengthen our relationship or end it. We had a choice to depend on each other or tear each other apart. While the story continues, several years away from our son's attempted suicides, my husband and I are still together.

Together does not mean we didn't struggle. The stress this has brought into our lives and marriage is beyond description. Luckily, it seemed that either I was strong and could help my husband, or he was strong and able to comfort me. We also quickly realized no one else knew what we were experiencing. We had this shared common bond. We could share our struggles and agony and even hope with each other in a way no one else could comprehend.

While every family dynamic is different, I share these examples as an insight. All people react differently. We all have our own ways of dealing with tragedy. Family, just like friends and acquaintances, will react differently to suicide and suicidal attempts. The bottom line is that you need to do what is right for you and your immediate family in dealing with these difficult situations.

Perceptions and Support

When a family member attempts or commits suicide, the rest of the family members are deeply affected. A variety of emotions come to the surface. These emotions are often heightened by how others react and respond to the situation.

We often feel judged. I certainly did. What did I do to make a child of mine want to end his life? While I know it was not me, on an intellectual basis, emotionally, I felt responsible.

We also believe that others look at us differently. Whether it is with sympathy, judgment, sorrow, or any number of other emotions, we believe there is a shift. It might be imaginary, but it feels real.

So many of these reactions seem as though they're directed at the family members. We feel as though we're under a microscope. We feel isolated. We

feel judged. We feel pitied. We feel responsible.
We feel broken. We feel shame. We feel
overwhelmed. We feel different. We don't even
know what we feel at times. Sometimes there is just
"nothingness."

We see the world moving around us. We put on
our happy faces and try to go about our lives. To
the outside world, no one would know that our son
had attempted suicide. The embarrassment, shame,
and guilt prevented us from sharing this with most
people, even close friends. Few knew of the chaos
that existed behind the doors of our home.

When family and friends are told of this type of
crisis, they often try to offer support and comfort.
Rarely do they know what we need. Rarely do we
know what we need. Many times, friends remain
silent not knowing what to do or say. Some might
blurt out things hoping to help but not having a
reference point, inadvertently make matters worse.

Some, who are affected, may want to talk and some may not. We are all affected differently, react differently and need support differently. My best advice is to tell your family and friends what you need. Often the best thing someone can do is sit quietly next to you and offer their presence – no words required. Remember, what you need may change as you go along your path and the process of grieving.

Stages of Grief

You might not think of grief when you think of depression, bi-polar disorder or having survived a suicide attempt. What is there to grieve; the person survived? Well, there is plenty. Grief can exist whenever there is a loss: loss of life, loss of a dream, loss of friendship, and so on.

First, let me review the commonly held stages of grief as offered by Elisabeth Kubler-Ross:

- **Denial:** Not wanting to face the loss; avoiding the reality.
- **Anger:** Anger at or about the loss (How could they leave you or how could this have happened?)
- **Bargaining:** If the person were alive, I would ... (Negotiation to undo or avoid the grief).
- **Depression:** Sadness over the loss, but also sadness for yourself.
- **Acceptance:** Realizing that you will be okay, even considering the loss.

When my son was taken to the hospital the first time he verbalized thoughts of suicide, and then again, when he attempted suicide, I experienced varying degrees of grief. When he was in the hospital, I wanted to deny the entire experience. At times, I was so angry that he had brought this upon our family. I certainly was depressed, at times, for myself and all I was dealing with regarding my son. Other times, I felt the loss of the hope and dreams I had for my son. Now, years after his attempt, I shift back and forth between Anger, Depression, and Acceptance. Most days, I can honestly say that I have accepted what has happened and what will always be a life of potential struggles for my son. Other days, I am just angry for all the pain we have experienced. It is normal to travel back and forth between these stages.

Guilt

There are so many times I have looked back over my life and my son's life and wondered why I didn't do things differently. If I had done _____, then_____. If I had not done_____, then_____. If I had been stronger, weaker, harder, lighter, more tolerant, stricter, more joyful, less optimistic … Wow! The list can go on and on. I have "mommy" guilt, Catholic guilt, and so much guilt in general!

Intellectually, I know my son's attempts at suicide were not my fault. Emotionally, I will always feel a little (sometimes a lot) of guilt. I could second-guess myself on every action and every thought and every spoken word. The reality is that, if a person is so fragile that they determine suicide is their only answer, it does not matter what others say or do. I am not saying we should not step in and try to intervene. Of course, we should try to prevent their choice to move forward with suicide. What I am saying though is that our words and actions are not the determining factors that lead the suicidal person to the conclusion that the only answer is to take their life.

We need to accept that we did not choose suicide for our loved one. Everyone is responsible for their own words and actions. While we can regret how we choose to act and speak, whatever our part, we did not choose suicide. We can, however, take responsibility, and even ask for forgiveness, for what we have said and done. Beyond that, we need to accept that any person who attempts suicide is dealing with so much more than what someone has said or done to them.

Statistics

So how common is suicide in the United States? Obviously, one is too many. The statistics are staggering. We don't know how many attempt suicide and survive. Ironically, more people are talking about suicide in this decade than ever before. We likely know someone who has been affected by suicide. I cite the following statistics to bring attention to the fact that it is a crisis and will likely touch many people directly or indirectly.

According to the Centers for Disease Control and Prevention, by the end of 2011, the U.S. was approaching 40,000 deaths from suicide annually. It's likely that number will continue to rise. Suicide is ranked 10th as a cause of death. The top means of suicide include firearms, suffocation, and poisoning. There is a higher rate of suicide from firearms in rural areas versus urban areas.

In a report from the American Association of Suicidology, based on 2010 data, and again gathered by the Centers for Disease Control and Prevention, men are more likely to complete suicide, but women are more likely to attempt suicide. Those in the 45-54 age group had the largest suicide rate. Suicide rates for married people are lower than those who are divorced, separated or widowed. There are higher rates of suicide with those who have a mental health diagnosis, especially depression, than the general population.

Warning Signs

Ironically, depression was not new to my extended family. I guess I just didn't want to see the possibility of it touching my immediate family. My paternal grandfather experienced severe episodes of depression and because of this was often hospitalized. I rationalized his experience as he had witnessed my grandmother's death when she was hit and killed by a drunk driver when I was only 12. I was an adult when my maternal uncle committed suicide. While I do not know if he was officially diagnosed with a mental illness, looking back I am sure he was struggling with several mental health disorders. He killed himself after my maternal grandmother's death of natural causes. His situation also seemed explainable as he had stolen hundreds of thousands of dollars that rightfully were willed to my mother and other family members. In both cases, tragic as they are, there were extenuating circumstances that seemed to offer explanations. There was a definite cause and effect.

In cases similar to my son's situation, there was no specific tragedy that caused his grief and depression. There was no simple explanation. Somehow, that makes it hard for me, as well as others, to rationalize how his depression could lead him to the extreme action of trying to kill himself. Unfortunately, that is often the reality when dealing with depression. For those of us on the outside, we just can't see the unimaginable pain depression can have on a person – pain so severe that they conclude their only escape is to end their life. Their pain is so severe that they seek death in all its finality.

There are signs and risk factors that are common among those who attempt suicide. They include, but are not limited to the following:

Saying "I hate myself."	Lose interest in activities
Any loss (job, relationship, etc.)	History of abuse
Lose interest in friends	Listening to sad music
Drawn to sad, dark images	Talking about death
Making attempts to say good bye	Risky behaviors
Giving away possessions	Threatening suicide
Planning suicide	Previous attempts of suicide
Mental health diagnosis	Terminal health diagnosis
Isolating self	Neglecting personal hygiene

If you see any of these signs or have any concerns about the mental state of someone, talk to the person. They may be reaching out for help. Sometimes, they just need someone to listen. Above all, seek professional assistance if you are concerned. This is not a matter of breaking trust or being disloyal. It may be a matter of life or death.

Getting Help

Obviously, when you are no longer able to function in life, you need to seek professional assistance. When you are physically sick, you go to your doctor. When you are mentally overwhelmed and not functioning, you need to seek a counselor or therapist. This applies to anyone you suspect is struggling with suicidal thoughts. It also applies to anyone who has lost a loved one to suicide or who has lived through the experience of a loved one who has attempted suicide.

One thing that helps is statements of affirmation. Find an affirmation that you identify with clearly and that "speaks" to your thoughts and feelings. Memorize it and/or write it down. Keep it with you to reflect upon when needed. Here are a few that might help:

- Today is a new day. Tomorrow is too.
- Life is fragile, I will be strong.
- I will live for the moment.

- I will focus ahead and on my future, not my past.
- Moment by moment.

While these are a few examples, take some time and find something that is meaningful and motivating for you.

The most important thing is to get professional help. Find a counselor or therapist.

There also many organizations that can provide valuable information:

American Association of Suicidology
(202) 237-2280
www.suicidology.org

National Suicide Prevention Lifeline
(800) 273-TALK
(800) 273-8255
www.suicidepreventionlifeline.org

American Foundation for Suicide Prevention
(888) 333-AFSP
(888) 333-2377
www.afsp.org

Suicide.org
(800) SUICIDE
(800) 784-2433
www.suicide.org

Also, look for support groups in your area. Groups like SOS (Survivors of Suicide) are located throughout the country. There are also groups for those who have attempted suicide and survived. Grief groups may also be helpful.

And Here We Are Now:

Five years after my son first attempted suicide, and several years after first publishing this book, I decided to add another chapter. The message all along has been one of hope. I initially began the journey of writing about my experience as an avenue for my own healing. After I started, I realized I had a message to share. It's not an easy message to hear, and not one many would feel compelled to read without good reason, but one that could offer hope to those who have experienced suicide, and the effects of suicide, in their own lives.

Since the first publication, many have shared how this book has helped them. There was a shared bond of experience. There was the offer of hope for a better future. There was understanding and there was acceptance.

My husband and Mitchell have not read the book. I don't believe they ever will. They don't need to – they lived the experience. My daughter and younger son have read it but don't talk about it. We still struggle some days. There will always be reminders. There is hope though.

Mitchell doesn't talk about that time in his life. In the future, he may want to but, for now, he is focusing on the future and finding his way in life. He is now more likely to identify when he becomes depressed. He takes steps to not allow himself to go to that 'dark place.' I will always worry that it will surface but I do not let it consume my thoughts and life. We all need to focus on the present and not let the past define us.

Mitchell recently moved out of our home. He moved states away to pursue a new fresh start. I am so very proud of him. He is facing life full on and finding his way. Again, hope is the guide!

Several years after Mitchell's attempt I heard about Project Semicolon. It is an organization founded by Amy Bleuel. As stated on their website www.projectsemicolon.com, "Within the belief that suicide is generally preventable, the mission of Project Semicolon is to help reduce the incidents of suicide in the world through connected community and greater access to information and resources. We believe that suicide prevention is the collective responsibility of each and every person on the planet." Just as a semicolon is a pause in a sentence, the semicolon represents a pause in a life. Today, people across the world have semicolon tattoos representing a 'pause' in someone's life who attempted suicide. Amy told her story, including her suicidal thoughts and attempts, and encouraged others to do so as well. She has been an inspiration to many. Sadly, even she lost in her fight with the disease and committed suicide in March 2017.

Marking Mitchell's journey, he and I went together to get semicolon tattoos. Both can be seen on the next page and on the back cover of this book. I have been impacted both personally and professionally with the horrific pain of depression to the point of suicide. If having a permanent emblem on my body is a means to spark a conversation with someone about suicide, I will have achieved a goal to bring awareness, help, and hope to those suffering with this disease. Personally, my tattoo – 'His story isn't over' – is also a reminder that every day with my son is a gift.

Amy Bleuel used her experience with suicide to help others. Even though she immersed her life in helping others, she could not save herself. Once someone has attempted suicide, statistically they are more likely to attempt it again. Through therapy they can explore their unique warning signs and have safety plans in place. Ultimately though, it is a struggle they need to monitor the rest of their lives.

Conclusion

I felt compelled to share my story. If I can offer some insight, comfort, knowledge, direction, it is worth it. No one should ever go through this alone. I know, both personally and professionally, it can make a difference when you speak to others who understand what you are going through. Yes, your story may be a little different, but having a common thread with someone else can provide comfort and reassurance.

Ironically, or who knows, maybe by destiny, one year before my son attempted suicide, one of my best friends called me to share her story. Her son, several years older than Mitchell, had attempted suicide. Luckily, he too survived. My friend and her family were devastated and she and her husband were struggling on how to move forward. She experienced much of what I have spoken about in this book. While she called me primarily because of my professional background, a year later I called her for her friendship and her ability to understand. While the boys had different issues, they both were dealing with depression. There were many common factors.

The strength both my friend and I gained from having someone understand what we each were going through is unbelievably critical. We held on tight to the reality that we were not alone. Yes, our spouses were present, and also striving to cope, but having someone outside of my specific experience, and yet able to relate completely, was of invaluable support to me. Now, years later, we still meet to share how we are coping and how our sons are functioning. There have been good times and bad times for all involved. We find comfort from sharing our experiences and knowing we do not judge each other but rather support each other in our journey.

I wish for you the same unconditional support.

Final thoughts:

1. While everyone who encounters suicide will react a little differently, it's very helpful to share with others who have experienced a similar crisis. When you are ready, talk to someone: a friend, a professional, probably both!

2. You are not to blame.

3. Suicide and attempts will change your family dynamics. You will need time to adjust. Each person may need to heal differently and that is OK.

4. After an attempted suicide, be on the watch for future attempts. Don't be afraid to speak to your loved one about his/her state of mind.

5. You have nothing to be ashamed of. Depression is a disease and needs to be seen as such. That said, there is no right answer as to whether you should share your story with others. Share only if it helps you in the process.

6. Be prepared to go through an emotional roller coaster. There will be grief over so many things. Healing and hope take time.

I wish you a life of happiness and the strength to endure. Seek help from friends, family, and professionals. Do what you need to do to cope. Never give up. Fight for the hope that tomorrow is another day.

Thank You

First, thank you to Lori for reading my story. She heard so much of my story as it played out and yet was willing to read, edit and critique it. Also, her photo editing skills are magic! Her friendship is invaluable.

I would like to thank Chris. She has been an example to so many on how to face life with courage and dignity. While life presented her with a challenge (and joy of a child with Down Syndrome) way before I knew the challenges that were about to so suddenly interrupt my life, her smile had demonstrated faith and love and determination.

Drawn together out of our love for our children and their education, while we were both PTO Presidents, little did we know that Dorothy and I would begin a friendship and bond that has sustained us in our trials and heartaches over the paths our sons have traveled. I can never thank her enough for her support, wisdom, and an occasional bed to escape a bad day and/or night. Of course, her editing is also something I am grateful for and I will forever be in her debt.

Thanks to my Chi Omega sister, roommate, and forever friend Susan. We were unlikely bunkmates because of our strong personalities but divine intervention surely put us together back at Bradley University. Sadly, our sons have experienced so much pain and her friendship and concern, and ever-present love have meant more than she will ever know.

Finally, this second edition was edited by Rich Rostron or Rich Publicity. While I enjoy his friendship, his professional guidance is greatly appreciated.

References:

On Death and Dying by Elisabeth Kubler-Ross, 5 Stages of Grief

American Association of Suicidology, Suicide in the USA, Based on 2010 Data

Centers for Disease Control and Prevention, Suicide and Self-Inflicted Injury, Http://www.cdc.gov/nchs/fastats/cuicide.htm